HOW TO PASS AN INTERVIEW SIMPLE GUIDE

Georgina Musembi

1

TABLE OF CONTENTS

CHAPTER ONE: INTRODUCTION

An interview can be defined as an attempt to secure the maximum amount of information from the candidate concerning his/her suitability for the job under consideration.

Limitations of Interview

- Interviews may not have clearly defined techniques developed thus results in a lack of validity in the evaluation of the candidates.

- There is always variation in offering to score to the candidates by the interviewers.

- Interviews can help judge the personality of the candidate but not the disability of the job.

- A single characteristic of the candidates found out on the basis of the interview may affect the judgment of the interviewers on other qualities of the applications (hallo effect).

- The brazenness of the interviewee may affect the objectivity of the interviewer.

- An interview is a time-wasting and expensive device of sample selection.

CHAPTER TWO: GUIDELINES FOR EFFECTIVE INTERVIEWING

- The interview should have a definite time schedule known to both the interviewer and interview.

- An interview should be conducted by competent trained and experienced interviewers.

- Interviewers should ensure an element of privacy for an interviewee.

- The interviewer should be supplied with a specific set of guidelines for conducting the interview.

- The resume/summary for the entire candidate to be interviewed should be prepared

- The interview should not end abruptly but it should come to a close tactfully providing satisfaction to the interviewee.

- Interviewers should show their sensitivity to the interviews sentiments and also a sympathetic attitude to him/her.

- Interviewers should also show emotional maturity and stable emotionality during interview time.

CHAPTER THREE: TIPS ON WHAT TO DO BEFORE AN INTERVIEW

The things to do before an interview are typically a bit more mental than anything else. Usually, the buildup to an interview is much more nerve-wracking than the actual interview itself. With that in mind, shift your focus to preparation and do whatever you can to practice relaxation beforehand! Nerves can be useful if they motivate you to act.

So take a deep breath, and read through the suggestions on things to do before an interview that will help you be prepared when you get into the room.

- **Get a good night's sleep the night before.**

You'll look better and feel better. This lets you make the best first impression.

Do your research.

Know the company that you are interviewing with so you can answer their questions well and in the right context. It will also show that you are truly interested in the company.

- **Eat a good breakfast.**

You'll be more alert and focused.

- **Prepare questions beforehand.**

Know the answers to basic questions that they will most likely ask you. Also, come up with a few questions about the company or position you are applying for to show that you're interested.

- **Make a few copies of your resume and the required documents**

Put them somewhere where you won't forget to bring them.

- **Search the web.**

It is likely someone else has interviewed with the company, so search the web and see what others are saying about it.

- **Make sure your clothes are clean and wrinkle-free.**

Know who will be interviewing you, and learn a bit about their background.

- **Know your strengths and put together a list of them.**

Prepare a solid list of references that you can give your interviewer on the spot.

- **Hygiene**

Brush your teeth.

Put on deodorant.

- **Pre-write your thank you notes so you can drop them off right afterward.**
- **Know how to answer the question, "What will you add to the company by joining it?"**
- **Carry a tissue or handkerchief in your pocket to dry your hands in case you are nervous before you go in.**
- **Turn off your cell phone.**
- **Prepare for the different types of interviews: behavior, experiential, or combination.**
- **Have a story from each place you've already worked at that exemplifies one of your strengths.**

For every strength or skill, you should have a story about how you successfully used it. You will make a far better impression if you can back up your dry list of previous employment with interesting stories that show what you gained from each experience.

You don't need to memorize everything on this list. Just make yourself familiar with them and you should be fine. While some of these should just be normal parts of your daily routine you would be surprised how stress can cause tons of people to forget these before a job interview.

Plenty of job-seekers who have taken pieces of this list and put it into a to-do a format on their phone or on paper.

This gives the morning of the big day some structure and allows them to feel confident walking out of the door. If you think that you're someone who might benefit from this, jot down this list of things to do before a job interview and check them off as you go.

No one ever suffered from being overly prepared!

CHAPTER FOUR: WHAT TO DO DURING AN INTERVIEW

Now that you're well-rested, prepared and at the designated location a little early – there are a few things to keep in mind once you're actually in the thick of things. Here's what to do during an interview:

- Answer the question that was asked.
- Shake the interviewer's hand.
- Let the interviewer show you your chair – now is the time to be submissive, so as to not offend the interviewer.
- Say "Yes," not "Yeah."
- Take a second before answering a question to show you are putting some thought into your answer.
- Take notes.
- Let your achievements speak for you.
- Ask questions, including asking for full descriptions of the type of work that you will be doing.
- Keep eye contact.
- Be yourself.
- Start with conversation topics that you are comfortable with. This will allow you to direct the interview to a certain degree and present yourself in a positive light.

CHAPTER FIVE: WHAT NOT TO DO DURING AN INTERVIEW

Make sure that you have at least a preliminary grasp of the no-nos. These can hurt or kill your chances of landing the job, and they are all very preventable. Make it second nature to avoid these and you will be in a very good spot when it's time to interview. This can help you make it past the first wave of interviews.

- Don't talk too quickly.
- Don't digress from your points. Answer the questions directly.
- Don't use slang.
- Don't use words you don't know the meaning of.
- Don't be arrogant.
- Don't talk about your personal life.
- Don't give the employer any reason to think you will not perform well.
- Don't act nervous. You probably will be, but it is best if you take a few seconds and clear your mind; your answers will be less jumbled. If you find yourself getting really nervous, excuse yourself and go to the bathroom to get some air.
- Don't take too long but it is better to collect your thoughts than to plow ahead when you can't focus.
- Don't fidget. This might be something you have to practice but it is worth it.
- Don't get defensive. The interviewer will be asking technical questions. Everyone has their weak spots and that is okay – work with it and practice for it.
- Don't bring coffee. Sipping a drink is a sign of disrespect during an interview.

CHAPTER SIX: WHAT TO DO AFTER AN INTERVIEW

First of all, take a deep breath; you've gotten through the most stressful part. While waiting for a response from the hiring manager can definitely be frustrating, knowing what to do after an interview can actually help you influence the outcome. Once you've accomplished these steps, you can rest assured that you did everything in your power to get the job offer.

- **Drop off your thank you note.**

Always, always thank your interviewer after you've left. Email them after you drop off your note. The more contact you have, the more you remain in their minds over the other applicants. It shows you're thoughtful, motivated, and that you care. The number of interviewers who leave and hope things go well is far too high when they could have more control of their fate by doing this after the job interview is complete.

- **Create a list of items that you did well and that you would like to improve on.**

This can be one of the most effective things to do after an interview because it will allow you to improve for future job interviews, or assess general weaknesses that will be helpful in your career. Doing this right after an interview is ideal as well because everything will be fresh. It doesn't have to be a big fancy list, bullet points will do. The most important thing to remember is to be brutally honest with yourself. Even if you didn't like the way the interview was conducted, there's always something you can do to improve. Find it!

- **Follow up appropriately.**

Sometimes the interviewer will tell you when they will notify you; other times it will be your responsibility to make the follow-up.

This is definitely one of the most important steps to remember regarding what to do after an interview. Sometimes things get crazy at work or papers and files get misplaced.

A gentle follow up after a while isn't going to hurt anything or make you seem desperate (something a lot of job-seekers have expressed concern with). If you were told there was a specific date to expect a response, wait until that date has passed and then reach out.

Managing what to do after an interview is more about keeping your nerves in check and following up correctly. Don't ever skip these steps because you think the job interview went terribly and there's no point, you really never know. We've heard from so many individuals that have thought the interview was awful and still got an offer.

Your mind can play tricks on you and exaggerate the smallest of mistakes until it seems like the entire process was a failure. Be confident, if you followed the earlier steps that we recommended you will be fine!

CHAPTER SEVEN: SIGNS YOUR JOB INTERVIEW WENT WELL

1. You're Asked About your Interest in the Job

Did the interview ask you what you thought about the job and the company? It's a good sign if your interviewer asks you questions about your interest in the job or where else you are interviewing. If she or he wasn't interested in hiring you, your desire for the job—or interest in other companies—wouldn't matter. Inquiries about your interest suggest the interviewer is considering whether or not you would accept a job offer.

2. Getting Specific About the Job Responsibilities

Did your interviewer dive into the specifics of the job and the daily responsibilities of the individual in that role? For an interviewer to take the time to get into the nitty-gritty can mean he or she felt confident enough about your capabilities to take the conversation to that level.

Bonus points if the interviewer referred to "you" in the role; for example: "*You* would be reporting to Martha, the digital marketing manager, each day." If the hiring manager is talking this way, it means he or she can foresee you in the role.

3. Your Interviewer Gives Positive Affirmation

If the interviewer provides positive feedback during the interview, you're on the right track. This can be an obvious but tell-tale sign of a successful interview. Listen to how your interviewer responds when you answer questions.

Positive responses like, "That's exactly right," "Great answer," or "Yes, that's just what we're looking for" are key indications that an interviewer likes you and will give your application further consideration.

4. You Get an Invitation for a Second Interview

With this one, it's easy to tell if the interview was a success. Getting asked to come in for a second interview is the best sign that your first one went well! Remember, though, don't let the news get to your head, as there is a good chance other candidates are also coming in for round two.

Embrace your confidence, but definitely, don't dismiss the need to prepare for a second interview just because you think you have the job in the bag.

5. Your Interviewer Sells You the Job

If the interviewer spends some time promoting the highlights of the position, the company culture, and why he or she loves working there, this is a good sign. Your interviewer probably wouldn't try to "sell" you the job if he or she had zero intentions of considering you for the position.

Another good sign is when an interviewer asks when you could start work if you were hired. Wanting to get an idea about when you can start is a good indicator that you're in contention for the job.

6. The Interview runs longer than 30 minutes

Did the interviewer spend time asking quality questions, listening to your answers, and discussing the details of the position with you? If you felt like you came away with a thorough idea of the position and your interview lasted for 30 minutes or more, consider it a good possibility that the interviewer was interested in hiring you.

However, in a case where there are multiple interviewers, however, one of them may feel the need to ask questions just to ask them in order to make it seem like they're doing their job. So, bonus points if it's just you and a single interviewer and the discussion still carried on for a significant amount of time.

7. Exchange of contact information

It is excellent news if your interviewer gives you a business card, or some direct line to reach him or her, like an email or even a cell phone number. Even better if he or she encourages you to reach out anytime if you have questions or concerns!

8. You're introduced to Staff

Consider it positive news if your interviewer toured you around the office and introduced you to staff. It's even better if he or she brought other staff members in during your interview for personal introductions and work-related discussions.

9. The Interviewer responds to your Follow-up

Once you've sent your thank you note expressing your gratitude for the interview opportunity, gauge how long it takes your interviewer or human resources contact to respond. A prompt response can be good news, but also keep an eye out for the tone of the message.

A message like, "Thank *you* for coming in to meet with us! We very much appreciate it and look forward to following up with you later this week. Have a great day!" bodes much better than something short and dry like, "You are welcome, and thank you. Speak soon."

10. Salary comes up

Most interviewers won't get into the (sometimes awkward) discussion of money unless they're serious about hiring you. Interview questions about your current salary, past salary, and what salary you are expecting to receive can be good signs that they are seriously considering you for the job.

If none of these things happen, remember that it might not because of anything you did or didn't say. There are many reasons candidates don't get invited for second interviews, and some of them have nothing to do with the applicant.

CHAPTER EIGHT: EASY-TO-MAKE JOB INTERVIEW MISTAKES

1. Dressing Inappropriately

When you interview for a job, it's imperative to look professional and polished. Although your attire may vary based on the position you're applying for — for example, you should wear business casual clothing to an interview for a non-professional job or startup casual garb to an interview at a small startup company — it's important to look well-dressed and put together, no matter what the company.

2. Arriving Late

Everyone knows that first impressions are very important in landing a job, but did you know that you can make a bad first impression *before* you even arrive at your interview?

Running late not only suggests poor time management skills, but shows a lack of respect for the company, the position, and even your interviewer.

Go the extra length to make sure that you aren't late, and arrive on time, or even early. Budget your time so that you make it to the interview five to ten minutes early. That way, if something unforeseen comes up on your way over to your interview, you'll have some cushion time.

3. Bringing a Drink With You

Ditch the coffee, soda, or water bottle before you enter your interview. If you need to fuel up, do it before you get to the interview.

Not only is it unprofessional to enter with a drink, but during your interview, you should be focused on the task at hand: making a good impression, answering questions, maintaining eye contact with your potential employer, and paying attention throughout the entire interviewing process.

Having a drink in front of you creates the opportunity for distraction — fiddling with the cup, or missing a question while taking a sip, for example. And although it may be a relatively unlikely possibility, bringing a drink into your interview also gives way to other unsightly accidents — like spilling the drink on the desk, on you, or even your interviewer!

4. Using your phone during the interview

Before you get to your interview, silence your phone. Texting during your interview is not only rude and disruptive, but it's a pretty clear message to your potential employer that getting the job is not your top priority.

For the same reasons, don't answer calls (and certainly don't make them) during the interview. To resist the temptation to check your phone, stow your phone in your bag before the interview. If you accidentally forget to turn it off, resist the temptation to check it if you get a message or call.

5. Not knowing anything about the company

Don't let your potential employer stump you with the question, "What do you know about this company?" It's one of the easiest questions to ace, if only you do some research before your interview.

Background information including company history, locations, divisions, and a mission statement are available in an "About Us" section on most company websites. Review it ahead of time, then print it out and read it over just before your interview to refresh your memory. Also check the company's LinkedIn page, Facebook page, and Twitter feed, if they have one.

6. Fuzzy resume facts

Even if you have submitted a resume when you applied for the job, you may also be asked to fill out a job application. Make sure you know the information you will need to complete an application including dates of prior employment, graduation dates, and employer contact information.

It's understandable that some of your older experiences may be hard to recall. Review the facts before your interview. If you need to, take the time to recreate your employment history, so your resume is accurate. It can be helpful to keep a copy of your resume for yourself to refer to during your interview, although certainly don't use it as a crutch.

Of course, you should never "fudge" any facts on your resume. The more truthful you are on your resume, the better you will be able to discuss your past experience during your interview.

7. Not paying attention

Don't let yourself zone out during an interview. Make sure you are well-rested, alert, and prepared. Getting distracted and missing a question looks bad on your part. If you zone out, your potential employer will wonder how you will be able to stay focused during a day on the job, if you can't even focus during one interview.

If you feel your attention slipping away, make an effort to stay engaged. Maintain eye contact, lean forward slightly when talking to your interviewer, and make an active effort to listen effectively.

While you may have no problem paying attention in a one-on-one interview in a private office, it's harder to stay in tune with the interviewer when you're meeting in a public place.

8. Talking too much

There is nothing much worse than interviewing someone who goes on and on. The interviewer really doesn't need to know your whole life story. Keep your answers succinct, to-the-point and focused and don't ramble—simply answer the question.

Don't get sidetracked and start talking about your personal life—your spouse, your home life, or your children are not topics you should delve into. No matter how warm, welcoming, or genial your interviewer may be, an interview is a professional situation—not a personal one.

Avoid this mistake by using nonverbal communication to impress your potential employer.

9. Not being prepared to answer questions

Your interviewer is probably going to ask you more than just the basics about where you worked, and when. To get a feel of your aptitude for a job, your interviewer is going to take advantage of the allotted time and flesh out everything he or she needs to know about you as an employee.

Don't let yourself be caught off guard. Prepare for your interview by reviewing questions to expect and how to answer them.

Be prepared with a list of questions to ask the employer so you're ready when you asked if you have questions for the interviewer. Review questions you should not ask during a job interview and the worst interview answers that you should avoid at all costs.

10. Badmouthing past employers

Don't make the mistake of badmouthing your boss or coworkers. It's sometimes a smaller world than you think and you don't know whom your interviewer might know, including that boss whom you think is an idiot. You also don't want the interviewer to think that you might speak that way about his or her company if you leave on terms that aren't the best.

When interviewing for a job, you want your employer to know that you can work well with other people and handle conflicts in a mature and effective way, rather than badmouthing your coworkers or talking about other people's incompetence.

When you're asked hard questions, like "Tell me about a time that you didn't work well with a supervisor. What was the outcome and how would you have changed the outcome?" or "Have you worked with someone you didn't like? If so, how did you handle it?" don't fall back on badmouthing other people. Instead, review how to answer difficult questions.

CHAPTER NINE: INTERVIEW QUESTIONS FOR TODAY'S RECRUITING LANDSCAPE

Today's recruiting environment has heaped unique and new challenges on the plates of human resource professionals and small business owners alike, particularly during the interview process. A flattened management hierarchy has increased the need for employees with the soft skills to self-manage and to work well on teams.

Add to that high unemployment, which has made work history gaps commonplace and the increased popularity of social media tempts some employers to examine candidates' social media history — a practice that can potentially lead to employment discrimination charges.

Recruiting the right candidate depends on knowing how to interview and to ask questions about these three current issues.

- **Soft-Skills Assessments**

When conducting an interview for soft skills, the best predictor of soft skills is information about how the person did in a previous job, says Jone Pearce, director of the Center for Global Leadership in The Paul Merage School of Business at the University of California, Irvine.

Choose a prior project or task mentioned on the applicant's resume and delve into the details by asking these behavioral interview questions:

What went well? What was the most rewarding? Does the candidate take credit for the success of the project or mention co-workers' efforts?

What didn't go well? What was frustrating? Candidates with poor soft skills will blame others for failure.

How did you go about getting the project approved? Whom did you approach, and how did you get that done? Does the candidate seek buy-in for new projects or go forward without permission and seek forgiveness later?

How were decisions made? Is the candidate's answer point to a team player or a lone wolf?

As the candidate answers these interview questions, screen for four characteristics that objectively indicate a job candidate's social skills:

- o Self-awareness of how actions affect co-workers
- o Sensitivity to the needs and feelings of others
- o Social intelligence and ability to influence co-workers
- o Self-control, particularly when under deadline pressure

- **Work History Gaps**

Given the condition of the overall economy, it's no longer uncommon to see job applicants with work history gaps. Knowing how to interview to uncover whether that work history gap was created by a poor economy or poor job performance is key.

Try these interviewing tips:

Start with a broad-based interview question: *I see you left your last position six months ago; what have you been doing in between?*

Follow up with a request for a reference: *Is there someone I can call at that company who can talk about what you did there and your experiences?*

When doing reference checking, start by asking a couple of references checking questions that open the door for the reference to say something nice about the candidate.

Can you remember one of the best things the candidate did? What was the nature of their job? Then, ask the same questions you already asked the job seeker.

"If the person is pausing a lot, ask who else you can call," says Pearce. "If they know someone is bad, they'll refer you to someone with a big mouth who will talk."

- **Body Language Clues**

Knowing how to interview often comes down to trusting what the job seeker says about their work history. Unless you hook candidates up to a polygraph, you can't determine whether the applicant is lying about their work history, but you *can* look for nonverbal clues that indicate distress, says Joe Navarro, author of *What Every BODY is Saying: An Ex-FBI Agent's Guide to Speed-Reading People.*

If you ask a tough interview question — *Would your last employer give you a recommendation, or would they never take you back?* — the job seeker may be uncomfortable because they had a terrible boss, or because they were a terrible employee.

Navarro offers these interview body language clues to watch for:

Does the candidate grab their jewelry, rub their neck or touch their collar? "If you see that, there are issues," Navarro says. "If someone's eyelids come down and remain low, they're bothered by the question. When the lips disappear, lip biting, lip compression, that's indicative of some sort of stress."

Another sign to watch for: prospective employees who are confident about gaps in their work history may put their chin forward when they answer tough interview questions.

- **Interview Questions about Social Media**

As social media use has exploded, the temptation to use social media history as part of the hiring background check has increased.

Resist the temptation — unless the job requires social media skills and your company has established social media recruiting guidelines.

Lori K. Long, associate professor and faculty fellow at the Center for Innovation and Growth at Baldwin-Wallace College, Berea, Ohio says her best-interviewing tip is this:

"Don't look at Facebook. If you explore Facebook, you're getting access to information about candidates that you don't want to know from a legal hiring perspective," she says. "If people have pictures of church activities and children that can creep into your decision-making."

There are few court opinions on the use of social media history in recruiting, and you don't want your company to be the test case in this area, she warns.

"There are other valid, more legally safe selection tools out there."

Long has two other social media history interviewing tips.

First, use professional social media – such as Twitter and BeKnown™ – to verify resume information and to recruit new hires.

And second, use it to network. "It's also a good way to know if there's someone in your organization who knows someone who knows the candidate to see if you can get any background information.

CHAPTER TEN: INTERVIEW TIPS FOR CANDIDATES

1. Practice and Prepare

Review the typical job interview questions employers ask and practice your answers. Strong answers are those that are specific but concise, drawing on concrete examples that highlight your skills and back up your resume. Your answers should also emphasize the skills that are most important to the employer and relevant to the position. Be sure to review the job listing, make a list of the requirements, and match them to your experience.

Note that even the most well-prepared response will fall short if it does not answer the exact question you are being asked. While it's important to familiarize yourself with the best answers, it's equally important to listen carefully during your interview in order to ensure your responses give the interviewer the information they are looking for.

Also, have a list of your own questions to ask the employer ready. In almost every interview, you'll be asked if you have any questions for the interviewer. It is important to have at least one or two questions prepared in order to demonstrate your interest in the organization. Otherwise, you might come across as apathetic, which is a major turnoff for hiring managers.

2. Develop a Connection with the Interviewer

In addition to indicating what you know about the company, you should also try to develop a connection with your interviewer. Know the interviewer's name, and use it during the job interview. (If you're not sure of the name, call and ask prior to the interview. And, listen very carefully during introductions. If you're prone to forgetting names, jot it down somewhere discreet, like in small letters at the bottom of your notepad.)

Ultimately, building rapport and making a personal connection with your interviewer can up your chances of getting hired. People tend to hire candidates they like and who seems to be a good fit for the company's culture.

3. Research the Company, and Show What You Know

Do your homework and research the employer and the industry, so you are ready for the interview question, "What do you know about this company?" If this question is not asked, you should try to demonstrate what you know about the company on your own.

You can do this by tying what you've learned about the company into your responses. For example, you might say, "I noticed that when you implemented a new software system last year, your customer satisfaction ratings improved dramatically. I am well-versed in the latest technologies from my experience with developing software at ABC, and appreciate a company who strives to be a leader in its industry."

You should be able to find out a lot of information about the company's history, mission and values, staff, culture, and recent successes on its website. If the company has a blog and a social media presence, they can be useful places to look, too.

4. Get Ready Ahead of Time

Don't wait until the last minute to pick out an interview outfit, print extra copies of your resume, or find a notepad and pen. Have one good interview outfit ready, so you can interview on short notice without having to worry about what to wear. When you have an interview lined up, get everything ready the night before.

Not only will planning out everything (from what shoes you will wear, to how you'll style your hair, to what time you will leave and how you'll get there) buy you time in the morning, it can help reduce job search anxiety, and it will also save you from having to make decisions, which means you can use that brain power for your interview.

Make sure your interview attire is neat, tidy, and appropriate for the type of firm you are interviewing with. Bring a nice portfolio with extra copies of your resume. Include a pen and paper for note-taking.

5. Be on Time (That Means Early)

Be on time for the interview. On time means five to ten minutes early. If need be, drive to the interview location ahead of time so you know exactly where you are going and how long it will take to get there. Take into account the time of your interview so you can adjust for local traffic patterns at that time. Give yourself a few extra minutes to visit the restroom, check your outfit, and calm your nerves.

6. Try to Stay Calm

During the job interview, try to relax and stay as calm as possible. Remember that your body language says as much about you as your answers to the questions. Proper preparation will allow you to exude confidence.

As you answer questions, maintain eye contact with the interviewer. Be sure to pay attention to the question so that you don't forget it, and listen to the entire question (using active listening) before you answer, so you know exactly what the interviewer is asking. Avoid cutting off the interviewer at all costs, especially when he or she is asking questions. If you need to take a moment to think about your answer, that's totally fine, and is a better option than starting out with multiple "ums" or "uhs."

Check out these tips on avoiding job interview stress to help keep your nerves calm. If the thought of a job interview puts you in panic mode, reviewing these interview tips for introverts will be a great place to start.

7. Follow-Up After the Interview

Always follow up with a thank-you note reiterating your interest in the position. You can also include any details you may have forgotten to mention during your interview. If you interview with multiple people from the same company, send each one a personal note. Send your thank-you email within 24 hours of your interview.

CHAPTER ELEVEN: INTERVIEW TIPS FOR EMPLOYERS

In today's labor market where unemployment is at an all-time low, preparing for job interviews has become essential. Not only does the process involve interviewing a candidate, but it also presents an opportunity for you to position your firm as an ideal employer.

Effective interview tips for employers focus on a wide range of factors. These include:

- Adequate preparation beforehand.
- Finding ways to engage the candidate on a personal level.
- Standardizing the interview approach for all candidates.
- Asking the right, open-ended questions.
- Watching out for job interview "red flags."

Here is a closer look at ways to tilt the odds in favor of finding the best candidate for your open position.

- **Be prepared**

Regardless of how good you are at talking off-the-cuff, a job interview isn't the place for a spontaneous conversation. Hiring teams or managers who "wing it" during an interview can come across as ill-prepared or not valuing the position (remember, the job candidate evaluates you and your company just as you're evaluating them). The individual seated across from you might be perfect for the job, but if they're turned off by the interview experience and decide to opt out, you'll never know.

It is important to verify information provided on a candidate's application or resume as part of an interview, but employers may be better served to prepare interview questions that shed light and insight beyond the applicant's professional persona as presented on paper.

- **Set the candidate at ease**

A job interview can be stressful. Don't look at the candidate's nervousness as an "advantage." By setting candidates at ease — something as simple as giving them a glass of water will do — this could help them be more comfortable and open about themselves, which in turn can lead to a more fruitful interview.

As you get started, offer a brief introduction of what you want to achieve, give an indication of the proposed length of the interview, and let them know there will be time afterward for their questions. Setting the scene is also a way to start building rapport with your potential employee.

- **Use the same criteria for each candidate**

Apply the same process and ask the same questions during each job interview. This approach enables you to gather information in a uniform manner and makes the next step — evaluating how well each person does — that much easier. It can also help minimize bias or other negative factors that may creep into the interview process.

- **Ask probing and open-ended questions**

Questions that invite a "yes" or "no" answer won't help you get beneath the surface with a promising candidate. Ask open-ended questions that invite people to open up about their background, ambitions, skills, and so on. Examples of such questions might include:

"Why are you thinking about leaving your current job?"

"What's the most rewarding experience you've had in your career?"

By listening closely to their answers, you can probe a bit deeper and learn more about what makes the candidate unique.

- **Ask follow-up questions**

As noted, open-ended questions offer the potential for insights into how a candidate thinks. But even they can be anticipated by a savvy job-seeker. Pay close attention to the candidate's initial answer to your open-ended question, but don't leave it at that. Ask follow-up questions that attempt to dig deeper into what the candidate has told you. This is the best opportunity to get an authentic, unrehearsed answer to your question.

- **Beware of questions you're prohibited from asking**

Certain potential interview questions are prohibited by state regulations and by the Equal Employment Opportunity Commission. Such interview questions could potentially make your company liable in a discrimination lawsuit.

For example, avoid any potential interview questions that touch upon an individual's race, ethnicity, or gender. Don't ask about the candidate's citizenship status or place of birth. Questions concerning religion or physical or mental disability should be avoided at all costs. The same holds true for inquiries related to a person's marital status or if a candidate is pregnant.

- **Keep detailed notes**

Don't try to evaluate how each interview went just on your memory alone. It's okay to take notes during the interview (politely explain to the candidate that you'll be doing so), but try to keep these notes to a minimum — whatever's needed to identify key facts and jog your memory later on.

- **Watch for non-verbal behavior**

A candidate's body language is often as informative as the verbal responses they give to your questions. Throughout the interview, keep an eye on their body language, how they sit, or their tone of voice in responding to questions. These observations can contribute to a more complete understanding of the candidate's potential.

- **Beware of certain interviewer errors**

We're all prone to making snap impressions of someone we meet for the first time, but it's best to curb that impulse during a job interview. Left unchecked, a first impression (good or bad) can cloud everything that happens afterward. Stick to the prepared questions and leave your snap impressions out of the equation.

Similarly, beware of the so-called "halo effect." This happens when a candidate's strong point (such as a prestigious school or a high-profile former position) colors the interviewer's experience. Any single fact shouldn't influence the entirety of the conversation.

- **Be on the lookout for job candidate red flags**

Many job seekers are genuinely motivated to do the best they can for their new employer. But a diligent business owner or hiring manager should be on the lookout for the few who don't merit serious consideration.

o Resume errors. This red flag can help screen candidates before they get to the interview stage. A professional resume (and/or cover letter) with clumsy syntax or typos can indicate a person who pays little attention to detail. Depending on the job qualifications, you likely want an employee you can trust to inspect and revise their own work before sending it on to others.

o Problems with communication. The open position may not require contact with customers, but virtually every position requires interaction with supervisors and other team members. Among the most valuable interviewing tips is paying close attention to how a candidate speaks, in addition to what they say. Some people will be anxious during the interview and talk too much — which could be a sign of poor listening skills that most employees need. They may also be talking a lot because they want to distract you from certain areas of discussion. In either case, this trait may not bode well for working as part of a team.

o An answer for everything. In a similar vein, a job candidate who glibly responds to every question can raise another type of red flag. No one's perfect, and someone who attempts to come across that way isn't being entirely honest. A desirable job-seeker is one who's willing to say, "I don't know" once in a while (though not too often).

o Boasts about job offers. In an attempt to come off as being in high demand, some job candidates may freely boast about other job offers they may have. This can send the signal they're willing to play one employer off another to get more money or job perks. Not only does this say something about a possible lack of loyalty, but it may also suggest they'll always be thinking about what else might be available in the job market.

○ What's in it for me? So-called "stepping-stone candidates" focus on salary and job benefits at the expense of inquiring about aspects of the open position. These individuals may be more interested in using your job opening to get a different position elsewhere. Clearly, this red flag shouldn't be ignored by an employer.

Conclude the interview on a positive note

Among the best interview tips for employers is the simple reminder: End the experience on a positive, upbeat note. Allow 10-15 minutes near the end of the interview for the candidate's questions. You can learn a lot by the types of questions an interviewee asks (if, for instance, they're heavily salary-focused, that could be another red flag), but it also offers the opportunity for you to "sell" your company and make the open position that much more attractive.

Finally, thank candidates for their time, offer some idea of when they'll be contacted about a decision, and show them out. Your friendly demeanor goes a long way toward making the interview a positive experience for everyone involved.

If you've found the right candidate, you may want to consider the next step of conducting a background check to make sure everything you learned about the potential new hire checks out. Read this article next to learn about the importance of this step in the employee screening process.

CHAPTER TWELVE: THE BEST OUTFITS FOR JOB INTERVIEWS

- **Professional / Business Interview Attire**

The first impression you make on a potential employer is the most important one. The first judgment an interviewer makes is going to be based on how you look and what you are wearing. That's why it's always important to dress appropriately for a job interview.

Generally, you want to wear professional, or business, attire. For men, this might mean a suit jacket and slacks with a shirt and tie, or a sweater and button down. For women, this might mean a blouse and dress pants or a statement dress. You can also incorporate some modern style trends into your outfit.

Whether you are a man or woman, you also want to think about the colors you wear for an interview. Avoid anything too bright or flashy that will distract the hiring manager.

- **Non-Professional / Business Casual Interview Attire**

If you have a job interview in an informal work environment, you might wear a business casual outfit. Business casual outfits are less formal than a suit, but they are also more professional and polished than, say, a t-shirt and shorts or a sundress and sandals.

Of course, make sure you know the dress code before you assume that business casual is acceptable. If you aren't sure, call the office and ask the administrative coordinator or contact the person who scheduled the interview for advice.

Always dress a bit more professional than the average employee at the company. If everyone is wearing shorts and t-shirts, for example, you might wear khakis and a polo shirt or button down.

- **Casual Interview Attire**

If you have an interview at a startup company, nix the head-to-toe formal business attire. Rather than showing up in a black suit and dress shoes, opt for something that is relaxed but still presentable: relaxed-fit khakis, dark-wash jeans, and a nice top, for example.

- **Best Job Interview Hairstyles**

There are lots of ways to style your hair for a job interview. While some options are funky and others are more traditional, remember that your hairstyle should not distract the employer. You will want your hair to be professional and polished, as your entire outfit.

- **How to Do Your Makeup for a Job Interview**

When you do your makeup for a job interview, it's important to make a good impression – without making too much of an impression by overdoing your makeup. Like your hair, your makeup should not distract the interviewer.

- **College Job Interview Attire**

While college students might dress casually in the classroom, they should dress professionally when interviewing for a professional job or internship.

Less formal is acceptable when interviewing for campus jobs and more informal workplace jobs. However, you still want to dress professionally for most positions, even if they are entry-level.

- **High School Interview Attire**

As is the case with any interview, it's important to look well dressed and put together even if you're a high school student looking for a part-time job.

- **Internship Interview Attire**

Internships are an important part of career development, and like any job, acing your interview is one part of getting the position you want. Making a great first impression – coming across as polished, professional and attentive – is important when it comes to your internship search.

- **Summer Job Interview Attire**

Are you interviewing for a summer job? Typically, these jobs are more casual and do not require professional attire. However, you still want to look polished and professional.

- **Interview accessories**

When you dress for an interview, how you accessorize is important. When wearing accessories to an interview, less is more. It's also important to choose accessories that will enhance your interview attire – not overwhelm it.

- **Interview Outfits for Men**

It can difficult to put a professional interview outfit together. While men may wear a blazer or suit jacket, button down shirt, suit pants, a tie and dress shoes. Business casual: Forget the suit when interviewing at a business casual company. Men might consider wearing a long-sleeved dress shirt, khaki pants a belt, and dress shoes.

CHAPTER THIRTEEN: WHAT NOT TO WEAR ON AN INTERVIEW

When you are dressing for a job interview, the image really is everything (or most of it). An unprofessional outfit can distract an interviewer from seeing your great qualities.

- **Keep bright, flashy colors to a minimum**

While everyone knows that short hemlines and plunging necklines aren't acceptable for a job interview, wearing an inappropriate dress that's also a bright, flashy color, like red, simply makes this situation worse.

So, be mindful when choosing your clothes. If you're going to wear a daring color do it tactfully, making sure the overall design of your outfit is especially conservative. There are other colors that are less dramatic that work well for business interviews. And, it's a good idea to avoid short hemlines and skin-tight fits altogether.

- **A blazer doesn't upgrade the rest of your outfit**

While a blazer is a good go-to choice for almost any interview, be mindful of what you wear underneath. Inevitably, the deep-v formed by the blazer's lapel creates a plunging neckline. If you're going to wear a camisole or a shell underneath, make sure it covers you appropriately. Of course, layering with a button-down is a no-fail option, too.

This tip applies to men, too. Unless you're interviewing in a casual environment, like at a startup company, wearing a blazer on top doesn't give you the excuse to wear a tired t-shirt underneath. Take the extra effort and put on a button-down or, at the very least, a V-neck sweater.

- **Go light on perfume and cologne**

Take it easy on the perfume and cologne, as you never know if your interviewer might have an allergy or aversion to strong scents. Either way, you don't want your overwhelming spray of perfume or dab of cologne to be the first or last, thing your interviewer notices about you.

- **Leave your headphones at home**

What's wrong with this picture? At first glance, it seems like not much, as the young man is dressed in a dapper suit and tie. But, take a closer look: the headphones have got to go.

While it's fine to listen to music on your commute to the interview, take them off before you enter the office, and stow them away before you're called in for the appointment. Otherwise, you risk seeming distracted and unfocused and you certainly don't want to be fumbling with tangled cords as you meet and shake hands with your interviewer.

- **Be careful about casual**

It can be hard to figure out what to wear for a summer job interview. When the weather is warming up, no one wants to suffer in a heavy suit. At the same time, that doesn't give you an excuse to throw professionalism out the window and wear super-casual shorts, a tank top, or a skimpy sundress.

Fortunately, because many summer jobs tend to be more "business casual" than especially dressy, most likely you won't have to dress in a dark wool suit or heavy blazer. Both men and women can consider wearing tailored khakis, a nice polo shirt or button-down, and a pair of sensible shoes but no flip-flops!

- **Avoid looking too dated**

In a competitive job market, everything matters - including your overall appearance. If your wardrobe is outdated, or if you have been out of the workforce for a while and your closet reflects it, invest in some modern, fashion-forward clothes to wear to your interview.

Don't forget about shoes, either. Throwing on a pair of sneakers, an old pair of pumps, or beat up dress shoes certainly won't make you look polished or professional. You don't have to spend a lot of money on your wardrobe, because you can easily find great pieces at discount stores like TJ Maxx and Marshalls, or even at stores like Target and Old Navy. You might be surprised by how much your shopping trip will pay-off.

- **Don't overdo your makeup**

While it's important to look your best, loading on makeup is not the best way to go about it. Keep your look natural, avoiding dark eyeshadow, bright lipstick, or heavy foundation. Your best bet is to stick with a light coat of mascara, a touch of powder, and some tinted lip balm. Aim to look refreshed and awake, without looking too done up. Interview makeup do's and don'ts will help you get the perfect look.

- **Traditional ties make the best impression**

Now is not the time to pull out that novelty tie you got last Christmas. Even if you think your tie will make a statement, err on the side of caution and stick with something that's more traditional. A pattern with conservative colors is perfectly fine--like subdued stripes or tasteful paisley--but don't try to be a funny guy who wears the tacky tie.

- **Keep accessories to a minimum**

Both women and men should keep accessories to a minimum. Ladies should avoid excess jewelry; instead of big hoops or chandelier earrings, opt for classic studs. It's also a good idea to avoid wearing flashy necklaces, large sunglasses, or anything "bedazzled."

While accessories aren't so much of an issue for men, it's important to be mindful of your cufflinks, your tie clip, and your belt; don't wear anything you might wear out to a club, for example.

Regardless of the accessories, you choose to wear, just remember that you want to look polished and professional. Don't let your outfit detract from the focus on the interview: you, your work experience, and how you would be the best fit for the job you want.

CHAPTER FOURTEEN: CONCLUSION

Purpose of Interviews

Most employers select people for jobs by giving them an interview. An interview enables an employer to decide whether or not you are suitable for the job on offer. It's also the perfect chance for you to ask questions and decide whether or not it is the type of job you think you would like.

Preparation is Key

You only get one chance to make a first impression so here are a few useful tips to help you get it the right first time. Before going for an interview, do your research. Check out the company's website or read relevant industry magazines. Knowing about the company and their business will show that you have the initiative, drive and are motivated by the company and the job. It will also help you to feel more confident during the interview.

Make sure that you are clear about your own interests and goals. Be prepared to explain why you want the job and why you think you would be suitable. Prepare and anticipate potential questions. This will help you to organize your thoughts and develop good answers. Know your CV inside out and be able to give specific examples to back up the information you have listed. Always treat a second interview or any subsequent interviews in the process as you would the first.

Don't Leave Home Without:

- Copy of your Curriculum Vitae
- References
- Examination Certificates
- Change for a parking meter if you're driving

- Contact numbers and directions to the company.

The Interview

Remember that it's perfectly normal to feel nervous about an interview. A certain amount of nerves can even help you perform better. Here are a few things you can do to help you feel more confident and improve your interview skills.

- Be sure that you read and know your CV in advance of the interview
- Be well prepared – know whom you are meeting and the interviewers' position in the company
- Research the company – always check their website
- Arrive early to allow time to compose yourself
- Dress appropriately – smart/professional
- Be polite to anyone you meet in the building
- Create a strong first impression, be polite and self-assured
- Make eye contact immediately when greeted
- Politely shake your interviewer's hand with a firm grip and a warm smile
- Wait for the interviewer to invite you to sit down
- Have an easy none work related topic of conversation ready to discuss
- Be relaxed but don't slouch
- Position yourself so that your body is facing the other person
- Watch your body language – look the interviewer in the eye and don't cross your arms
- Let the interviewer lead the conversation
- Listen carefully to the questions being asked and ask them to repeat or rephrase the question if you are unclear

- Be honest and objective whilst answering questions and maintain good eye contact throughout the interview
- Answer what you have been asked and try not to go off on tangents
- Do not interrupt the interviewer
- If you are interested in the position, make sure they know
- Thank the interviewer for taking the time to meet with you.

Avoid...

- Answers that are too short
- Being negative
- Providing detail or information other than what is required
- Becoming frustrated or uneasy when asked stressful questions
- Making derogatory or negative statements about former employers
- Misrepresenting your skills, experience or educational background
- Poor body language
- Using offensive language.

Questions You May Be Asked...

- Tell me about yourself
- What do you do in your present position i.e. duties and responsibilities?
- What do you like about your job?
- Is there anything in your present job you would prefer not to do?
- Why do you want to leave your present position?
- What are your weaknesses/best qualities?
- How would your immediate supervisor describe you?
- Where do you see yourself in three years' time?

- How do you work/interact with others?

Employers should not ask you what salary you require, however, this can be a tricky question, so always ensure you are armed with the current market rate and what your last salary was (if you feel that will give a good indication of your expectations), and a ballpark figure of what you would be happy to accept, but always be realistic!

You can also say that using your skills in the role, progression opportunities and looking at the overall package (healthcare, pension, etc.) are important considerations for you, i.e. not just salary.

Questions You Can Ask...

At the end of the interview, you will be given the opportunity to ask additional questions. Develop some that will help you understand the job's parameters and potential e.g.

- If I am successful in securing this position what are the 3 most important tasks I need to work on?
- What training opportunities are available?
- Do my skills and experience match those needed to fill your vacancy?
- How would you describe the culture of your organization?

Closing the Interview

It's very important to end on a positive note and reiterate your interest in the role, ensure you say something along the lines of 'I really like what I have heard about the company and I feel this is where I would like to work if given the opportunity. Is there anything I have said today that you'd like clarification on?'

Thank them for meeting you, give a firm handshake with good eye contact and don't forget to smile!

After the Interview

You may not be told straight away whether or not you have got the job. Other applicants may have to be interviewed or the employer may have to consult other people in the firm before reaching a decision. On the other hand, you may be offered the job on the spot. Do not accept the job if you have no intention of starting it.

Conclusion

While you may think that you are fairly adept at interviews, you will get better with practice. Generally, it takes two to three interviews before you become comfortable with answers and you respond in a natural way. It is critical that you are well prepared and practice interviewing skills prior to interviewing for any position that you really want. The more you prepare, the better the impression you'll make on the people you meet and the more you will increase your chances of securing a job offer. If you would like some one-to-one advice before your interview please speak to your consultant.

www.ingramcontent.com/pod-product-compliance
Lightning Source LLC
Chambersburg PA
CBHW030736180526
45157CB00008BA/3197